To the millions of stars who have fallen
to planet Earth.
May you shine ever so brightly!
And to the five little stars whom I plucked
from the heavens and named
Carl, Nicholas, Alexander,
Christopher and Coleman

All quoted material, prefacing the description of each sign, was generously given to me by my eternal friend, Steven Labensart, from his collection of musical lyrics, which define the beauty of his truth as I, among many, experienced it.

Reflections of
Consciousness

Also by Jessie Gresham Zapffe

DARK PLACES, LIGHT PLACES
A novel of love . . . and grace

Reflections of Consciousness

Jessie Gresham Zapffe

Foreword by
Jeff Green

sunfire productions
PO Box 1289, Mt Shasta, Ca 96067

ISBN 0-9624139-0-9
Library of Congress Cat. #90-070328

Cover and book design by PanDesign, Mt Shasta, Ca
Typesetting by Kim Solga Artworks, Mt Shasta, Ca
Printing by McNaughton & Gunn, U.S.A.

Acknowledgments

This little book has been a gift of Spirit, conceived in a meditation and completing itself with me as its scribe. However, it would never have come into its present state without loving help from my friends. To each of these special people, I offer my love and gratitude:

Alan Mainwaring who was there from the beginning, and who helped me bring it down to earth; Pan Brian Paine who did the cover and all of the art and whose expertise created the format; Neera Brechmann-Auer who, with Pan, gave me many valuable suggestions and tremendous encouragement; Alan, Pan, and Neera for their fearless editing, regardless of my reaction (perfection is never immediate!); Kim Solga and Linda Rose of Kim Solga Artworks who just know how to do it right; Jeff Green who so generously offered to write a foreword; and my sister, Carlotta K. Tutor who has always been there for me, when I am about to go under, with those ten little words: "I love you and the check is in the mail!"

*jg*z

Foreword

In this new book REFLECTIONS OF CON-
SCIOUSNESS: THE ZODIACAL JOURNEY, Jessie
Zapffe has managed to present the essential
archetypes for each of the signs. Archetypes, if
understood, allow for a comprehension of the
structural totality of consciousness.

So much is written in astrology that
emphasizes this characteristic, or that trait, that
the essential psychological dynamics are lost, or
simply not presented. The progression of human
development reflected through consciousness as
it evolves is simply ignored by most. As a result
many students of astrology are reduced to
memorizing lists of characteristics and traits with
no understanding of the *BASIS* of those
characteristics or traits. This does not allow for
any true perception at all, and produces fuzzy
minded astrologers who are at the mercy of the
various authors who present astrology in this
way. Consequently, creative or inspired self-
realizations about the nature of the astrological
archetypes, as reflected through the signs, does
not occur.

Reflections of Consciousness

In this very succinct and well written treatise, Jessie allows the student to grasp the essential meanings of the archetypes, and as a result, allows the student to reflect for himself upon these meanings in such a way as to lead into a creative state of self-reflection, which allows for an expanded awareness as to the nature of astrology and life itself. Read, reflect, expand, and enjoy.

God Bless,
Jeff Green
Lopez Island, Washington
USA

Author's Note

Within each of our individual charts is a microcosmic pattern of energy which represents the issues the soul has set forth for itself while experiencing life in the physical vehicle. It is not that one is born an Aries or a Libra, but that one embraces particular energies from several signs whose dynamics, as seen within the chart, interplay with one another as the life drama unfolds.

Thus it is that the consummate wo/man is a composite of energies which have been orchestrated in such a way that they are directly related to the evolutionary growth of the soul. As no two charts are alike, neither is one person as another, for each one's chart dynamics are externalized through experiences which are created specifically for his individual path.

Even in the case of twins who share the same chart, there is a unique soul expression for each twin, when the whole of the chart is made dual in that it might serve each soul. In this case, the astrologer must intuit which energies apply to which twin.

Author's Note

It is impossible for an astrologer to isolate one particular energy within the chart and to proclaim this as the person, for to do so would imply that there is an equal relationship among all people in terms of karmic lessons. For example, there are generations of people born with planets in a particular sign. As a group, there may be a common goal; however, individually, that goal's significance can have an extreme variation. Energies create the man. The vibrational pattern of each person is reflected through the composite energies he carries with him, and this is indicated by the whole chart, rather than any one aspect.

Likewise, one cannot look at the chart on a mundane level without giving equal time to an esoteric perspective The energy of each planetary placement within the chart carries with it a vibrational level which can range from one of coarse density to pure energy, in relation to the evolutionary stage of the individual. Someone may be highly developed in one area of his expression, while still struggling with baser energies in another. We become like Gods through first becoming human.

Only the soul knows that which is its destiny. It is the Inner Being, at the very heart of the soul, who guides one to the outer experience.

Consciousness expresses and defines itself through the human form, and the astrological makeup of any one being is a reflection of Consciousness that is unique unto itself.

jgz, Mt Shasta

Contents

"AS ABOVE, SO BELOW"

We are
Reflections of Consciousness

ARIES
21 Mar – 20 Apr

"I Am"

Cardinal Fire   Masculine   Mars   The Ram
Garnet   Amethyst   Bloodstone

*"Golden fires burning, bejeweled warriors shivering -
Ride the dragons across the skies! Ride to the battle
with Victory's cry!"*

It is under the sign of Aries that the Word is
made flesh. Consciousness, or God, existing
in a state of unity, does not know itself. That
it might have a sense of it's own uniqueness,
God creates form for itself and enters the
world of duality, that it might know the
answer to the question: "Who am I?"

Thus, in Aries, God leaves the realms of
formless non-being and enters the world of
being. It is to be remembered that the mind
creates a *sense of beingness* through its dual
perception of "you" and "I," as opposed to

[1]

the state of the Absolute in which there is only "I", with no sense of identity. There is no separation in this condition for comparison. All is One.

The very energy of Aries is one of the fiery Spirit, forced to tame itself in a world of matter. As this energy dilutes itself, through its movement around the wheel of Karma and Rebirth, it will ultimately return to its original state in Pisces. The color red, often associated with Aries, is the very color of life itself, - the fiery creation.

Where Aries lies within the chart, there is the need to know the answer to the question: "Who am I?" on a very basic level. This energy is often childlike and quite egotistical, for Aries lacks the logic to define itself from within. Rather, Aries seeks to know itself through that which is *external* to itself.

The fiery spirit of Aries develops its self-awareness, and creates its perimeters, through the response of the environment to its actions. This response varies, in accordance with the law of reciprocity. As energy is expended, so must it complete itself through a circuitous path of equality.

This need for *self-definition* is what motivates Aries, either consciously or unconsciously, even to the point where it is blind to that which is beyond itself. As with a small child, there is a zeal which is expressed spontaneously and then refined through external influence.

Here is the purity of the primordial energy in its raw and untampered state! Thus it is that Aries' actions are born of instinct, rather than logic. It is said that many centuries ago, a certain country, when needing to defend itself from invasion, sent out those men into battle who were born under the signs of Aries and Scorpio. For where instinct propels, fear is not known. Where blind zeal directs, logic does not exist.

The Arian fires burn spontaneously and unself-consciously. Consequently, Aries can be caught in its own conflagration, often developing awareness through hindsight. There is no residual ember smouldering beneath the surface. Aries energy expresses itself *impulsively*, and *without guilt*, for until it

[3]

reaches maturity, it does not apply reason to action.

This impulsiveness often moves Aries to externalize responsibility, to firmly insist that others are to blame. There is a magnified sense of "me" versus "you", as Consciousness awakens to the illusory state of separation from its original unity.

When Aries energy becomes refined, through a growing sense of human awareness, it can begin to express its dynamism through focused channels. There is an exceptionally high level of creativity within Aries, although it will not sustain itself without this maturity.

Aries is the proud warrior, the champion of life, ready to go into battle for its ideals! Ever awakening to new levels of creativity and filled with the *light of enthusiasm*, Aries will tirelessly thrust itself forward, open to its fate, as it initiates its path on the zodiacal wheel!

Note: The rulership of Mars and Aries relates to the use of the personal will expressing itself

[4]

without the wisdom of the soul to guide its actions. Aries is assigned to the First House in the natural zodiac, and it relates to one's personality, one's physical being, one's outlook on life. Aries rules the head.

Whatever sign is on the cusp of the First House, or the Rising Sign, will have an underlying Arian energy to it. As Mars initiates its actions through instinct, so will the Rising Sign express itself through instinctive action, rather than action provoked by forethought. As the personality moves into attunement with its soul purpose, it is expressed through the energy of the Rising Sign.

Reflections of Consciousness

"I Build"

Fixed   Earth   Feminine   Venus   The Bull

Gold   Jade   Coral

*"The singleness of Nature's
course draws my simple life."*

The unrestrained energy of Aries *grounds* itself in Taurus. It is as though Spirit suddenly becomes aware of itself through a newly developed sense of *body consciousness*. With the attention now focused on the *physical vehicle*, there is initiated at the very core of all Taurean energy, a strong element of survival. Once consciousness becomes fixed within the corporeal reality, it succumbs to the illusion of that reality and attaches itself to the flesh, blood and bones which give it form. Externally, this is

[7]

manifested through a desire to give the body a sense of well being through the creature comforts, for there is security, as well as self-definition, in this.

This fundamental survival instinct demonstrates itself on very subtle levels, as Taurus uses its *will* to create a sense of personal security in a world that does not offer it. Taurus will place a rather tenacious hold on that which it feels to be a necessary accoutrement to its existence, until either its needs have been met, or until resistance on the other end proves to be unrelenting. It is to be understood, that this survival instinct is motivated by a certain subconscious fear which is engendered by the attachment to the body.

Taurus has a natural affinity for all that which the physical plane offers. Hence, there is an attraction to food, music, and anything which can be manipulated by the hands to create something such as carpentry, gardening, - even painting. It is a natural law of attraction, in that these very things are associated with the ultimate comfort of the body. Often, Taurus will create for itself a large physical vehicle to accommodate its desires.

Where Taurus is found in the chart, there is a strong need for *self-reliance*. It is of utmost importance for this energy to *manifest its needs* on the physical plane. In spite of the fact that it is a feminine sign, Taurus needs to work with the *masculine aspects of self* in order to carry out this instinctive desire. The duplicity, and often secretive nature, that can be associated with this sign is the result of the negative feminine who, unable to create a form for its receptivity, turns inward in a pattern of self-destruction.

The self-sufficiency, which Taurus seeks to create, is related to the deep rooted need it has for security. For example, one's own success becomes a tangible reality belonging *solely to one's self*. To others, it offers an elusive, yet magnetic, attractiveness, thereby affirming Taurus' sense of security. As Taurus matures, the same sense of well being will emerge from that which it develops internally, rather than that which it has created in the outer world.

[9]

There is also a strong sensuality that is naturally related to Taurus. The instinctive motivation for survival expresses through the desire for this energy to reproduce itself. On an elemental level, this will reflect itself through the taking of a mate to bring forth children. When, however, this force is expressed differently, the creativity associated with children is redirected, thus bringing forth fruits of a different nature.

The feminine and the masculine within one will join together to create a vehicle that will give Taurus the sense of *self reliance* it needs. This, in turn, alleviates the role of the survival instinct, which has served as the major impetus in activating the inner power to realize itself externally.

At this point in its development, Taurus will have all of the security it needs. It will have become attuned to the nature of the corporeal reality, thus allowing its *receptivity* for the shift to the mental plane in Gemini.

Taurus: *April 20 - May 21*

Note: The rulership ascribed to this sign, is that of Venus, and it is mirrored in the Taurean love of beauty in the World of Form. Taurus is associated with the Second House of possessions, resources, personal desire, and financial security. Physically, Taurus relates to the throat, or the creative center.

Reflections of Consciousness

[12]

GEMINI
II
21 May - 21 June

"I Think"

Mutable   Air   Masculine   Mercury   The Twins
Emerald   Aquamarine

*"In Duality's cause, Mind appears
and obscures the Tao."*

As Aries relates to the Spirit made flesh and its self-definition, Taurus corresponds to the physical vehicle with its fundamental needs, and Gemini identifies with the mental body. Thus, we have threefold man - Body, Mind and Spirit - all associated with planetary entry. Aries relates to "me", Taurus to "mine", and Gemini to "I think, therefore I am."

In a sense, it is for Gemini to *transcend* the mental process. With Gemini, there is an insatiable thirst for knowledge. It is in this

[13]

sign that the ego becomes fully immersed in the world of matter, for with Gemini, the fall into Duality is never more apparent. Hence the ascription of the Twins to this sign.

If indecision is attributed to Gemini, it is because there is an inherent pattern to accept all knowledge as truth, and to see the truth in duality. Ultimately, as this energy matures, Gemini learns to see the truth as it pertains to itself, rather than accepting at face value that which others proclaim to be the truth. There is within Gemini the need to bridge the world of concepts, to synthesize knowledge into truth, and to see the underlying unity in that truth.

It is in Gemini that the capacity for mental dexterity is at its strongest. The mind, wishing to remain within the safety of the conceptual world, adapts to the illusion of it. Very powerful aspects of Gemini, or this mental energy, will override the intuitive process time and time again, as the illusory power of logic can be overwhelming to the gentle voice of intuition. The strength behind Gemini's opinions is directly related to the carefully fabricated stronghold of credibility it has given to worldly knowledge.

It may seem at times, that Gemini is insensitive to others, particularly when relating on an emotional level. The mind seeks to distance itself from the emotional body, finding no security in that which appears to be so fickle, yet containing such "abysmal" depths. To Gemini, there is a comfortable superficiality in all knowledge that precludes experiencing the depths of the soul. However, these depths must be reached, *through the emotional realms*, before knowledge can be transformed into wisdom.

The mercurial nature of the Gemini mind seeks to root itself in the security of knowledge, and as the true nature of security dwells in the very center of the soul, Gemini will attempt to ground itself, with a fierce regularity, to that which has no substance. For all knowledge comes from the world of illusion, and illusion will not hold itself in the face of Truth.

The saving grace of Gemini is its wonderful openness, its mutable nature. It is able to look

[15]

at itself with such remarkable candor, accompanied by a willingness for change. Swift footed Mercury cannot carry dross matter, as he moves through time and space. Consistently, Gemini will shed its old clothing for new, will release old concepts for new ideas, and will move on to the next challenge.

Wherever Gemini lies within the chart, there is an opportunity to open to new levels of knowledge, to expand concepts that may be limited. Through reciprocity in communication with others, one can open to the excitement of growth through diversity!

The all consummate challenge for Gemini is to *annihilate the mind*, for the mind is the labyrinthian maze in which one might lose one's self before ever connecting to the Absolute. In truth, the mind will ultimately seek to destroy itself, for it is constantly seeking answers to the question: "Why?" It will not stop until it has peeled back all of the layers, only to arrive at the center where he who asks (Gemini) and He who Knows (the Self) are found to be one and the same. It is at

[16]

this point in the evolution of the soul, that the mind dissolves itself into the Absolute. Here, there are neither questions nor answers, for All simply Is.

Herein, Gemini simultaneously finds the *true nature of security* and loses its need for it. The Truth which Gemini has consistently sought, externally, is not to be found further than the center of one's own being! "Center everywhere! Circumference nowhere!"

Preparation can now be made for the next step in the soul's evolution, as it begins to create an emotional body for itself, under the sign of Cancer.

Note: Mercury, the Communicator, is the ruler of Gemini and the Third House, which relates to the acquisition of knowledge, communication, duality, the power of the conscious mind, brothers and sisters, writing, speech, memory, early education, and short journeys. Gemini rules the nervous system, the arms, the shoulders, the hands and the lungs.

[17]

Reflections of Consciousness

[18]

CANCER
21 June - 21 July

"I Feel"

Cardinal   Feminine
Water   The Moon   The Crab
Pearl   Moonstone

*"I console as the mother, then I am born
as the helpless babe."*

In the sign of Cancer, one leaves behind the world of the mind for the emotional realms. It is now time to create a *self-image* through a proper balance of the mental, the physical, and the emotional bodies. The first six signs - Aries, Taurus, Gemini, Cancer, Leo, and Virgo - relate to the *subjective* world of wo/man. Spirit, having chosen a physical vehicle for its self expression, must initially come to terms with its own self, before it can relate to the objective world. In Cancer, the energies of

[19]

Aries, Taurus, and Gemini are internalized to create a strong self-image, which will be used as a foundation from which one will later relate to worldly matters.

As the moon, unable to sustain itself with its own light, reflects the light of the sun, so does Cancer have the tendency to reflect that which others might bring to her, without giving definition to that which she already is. Before she can step into the limelight of Leo, Cancer must seek to understand herself on a feeling level, thus engendering for the first time a relationship to the emotional body.

That it might find a sense of inner security, Cancer will attempt to create for herself the illusion of security externally. As the crab has its shell in which to retreat, so must Cancer find a comfortable solitude in her sur-roundings, leaving them behind when she feels the outer environment is non-threatening.

There is a need for this sign to nurture itself first, and then to bring that nurturing energy to others. Cancer correlates to the Mother, to the receptive feminine. Those whose charts reflect a strong Cancer will often carry a nurturing energy field. While others are instinctively drawn to this energy, the one who carries it may not have developed sufficient awareness of it, still seeking consolation from others, instead of learning to give and to receive from the Self.

Western society has traditionally defended the supremacy of masculine energy, while its feminine counterpart has been ignored. Great love and respect has been lavished upon male deities, saints, and leaders, and to their words and deeds, thus creating an exaggerated imbalance with the masculine. This attitude is not unique to society as a whole, for individually, we have also neglected to embrace and to revere the feminine.

In Cancer, one has the chance to understand the all-embracing, receptive feminine archetype, after one has come into a balanced state with one's emotional body. However, to the preceding signs of Aries, Taurus, and Gemini, the emotional world presents itself as a vast, ominously absorptive

[21]

dark sea. To fall into this void would be analogous to drowning.

When this type of fear provokes one into repressing or ignoring the *energy* of emotions from releasing itself, crystallization of form occurs. Initially, this is reflected in the eyes, as a type of hardened anger, before it manifests itself elsewhere in the body.

Working with the energy of Cancer, one must learn to balance giving and receiving, nurturing one's self and nurturing others. Often, this energy will express itself physically in the form of a rounded belly (the womb), or a round face (the moon). The depression that is characteristic of this sign is nature's way of bringing forth an understanding of the emotions, - to teach one the lesson of discernment between that which is his own feeling state and that which belongs to another. For of all of the signs, Cancer has the greatest intuitive capacity. Like a sponge, she draws everything to herself, losing her own definition as she fills herself with everyone else.

The depression can also be the quiet voice

of the feminine asking to be received, asking one to merge into her. Analogously, the earth receives that which animal and man impress upon it, only to continually bring forth of herself, through the regenerative/creative process, that which is ever new. She remains ever in the unchanging balanced state of giving and receiving.

Thus it is with Cancer, that one comes into one's own destiny through this same equilibrium. As the nurturing quality may initially demonstrate itself through cooking, or the comfort of a home, ultimately, there must be a transformation into that very state of beingness of the intuitive, all consolate Mother, embracing others with the warmth and the depth of her soul.

Wherever Cancer lies within the chart, there is the chance for one to open to his intuitive side and to more clearly understand the emotional body. It is the opportunity for one to embrace the feminine archetype, receiving and giving from the inner Mother.

As with the crab who shyly steps forward and then retreats, so it is with Cancer that

[23]

there might be an underlying fear in putting one's self on the line, in opening to the exciting diversity of life. Yet it is for Cancer to know, that she carries a natural protection which emanates from the very source of her being, from its very depths, and that this protection, this inner security, to which others are drawn for solace, is eternally there to be received by herself as well!

Note: The Moon is the ruler of Cancer and the Fourth House which relates to the emotional depths, self-image, one's home life, matters of real estate, and the parent of the opposite sex, or the least dominant parent. The Moon and Cancer rule the breasts, the stomach, and the solar plexus.

"I Will"

Fixed   Fire   Masculine   The Sun

Diamond

"What will remain of me?
Once the flame is lit, the heart will never die."

In the cycle of life, through the sign of Leo, it is the mother who is reborn to know herself as the playful child. With the composite energies of Aries, Taurus, Gemini, and Cancer, there is within one, a sense of completion that invokes the desire to project (it) out into the world. This projection becomes the stage upon which Leo will stand to present himself, eventually demonstrating his individual role in society.

It is not the nature of Leo to come into the world knowing what this function is. Rather, it is for him to awaken to his own uniqueness. Thus it is that Leo may appear to be entirely self-absorbed, yet this *self-focus* is necessary so that he may define the role which he will ultimately portray on the stage that is life.

At Leo's core is a keen sensitivity to external reaction. Although he presents the facade of a strong self-image, this often appears to others as childish egotism, causing them to withhold the accolades that Leo inwardly desires. Forever seeking to know his own worth, through the positive response of the world around him, Leo flamboyantly holds his mask for others to see, while trying it on for size.

As the Sun is the center of our universe, so must Leo be the center of his, whether he be introvert or extrovert. There is a certain light that children carry with them, a gift they bring into the world from other realms. It is that very light of the Sun which can blind those who are not protected by the wisdom of the soul. It is the light behind the personality, *in its purest expression*, for the spontaneity of the child is not inhibited by reason. As the child grows into an adult, that light becomes obscured by layers of experience which Leo must penetrate, that it might again reflect the radiance of the Sun.

For Leo is the sign of the heart, the center of our physical vehicle, and it is the destiny of Leo to awaken to the light of the soul through the process of developing his self-love. This is Leo's greatest struggle, learning to love the Self, and then opening the heart in love to others.

There can be a certain selfishness reflected through Leo's actions. The fixity of the sign provokes an attachment to that which one feels is essential to his needs. Even the generosity ascribed to the royalty of Leo is controlled by this attachment. When Leo discovers his own gift, the Light of his Being, he will know that it can be given freely without ever showing signs of depletion. Likewise, he will cease to look to the response of others as a mirror of his worth.

Thus it is that Leo needs to focus on awakening to the source of his individuality, and eventually, to express that uniqueness

[27]

through his creativity. Wherever Leo falls in one's chart, there is the need to become one's own *authority* over one's destined form of expression! In Taurus, there was the natural urge to reproduce the species. In Leo, the urge is to reproduce the spark of the Self through *the creativity of the soul!*

This is indeed a sign of initiation, as Leo must pass through the trials of walking a difficult path to place its own star in the heavens. It is not easy to become like the Sun, and yet within Leo is the energy of the will and the strength of focus, that he might assume his true role, and through the vivacity of his personality, play it well. The secret is in a proper balance between the *right use of will* and the *activation of the love principle.* The self-absorptive child matures into the loving adult who, having lit the flame of his heart, becomes the sunbeam for others. As Leo has become aware of his individuality, he now looks to Virgo for synthesis.

[28]

Note: The Sun is the natural ruler of Leo and the Fifth House which relates to self expression, children, drama, theatre, gambling, and love affairs. Leo rules the heart and the spine. The fire of the kundalini rises up the spine and awakens one to the Beloved who dwells within the heart.

Reflections of Consciousness

Mutable Earth Feminine Mercury The Virgin

Pink Jasper

"Rose Light, bathed in pure white,
Behold the crescent dawn."

In Leo, the individual essence has been defined, and in Virgo, rather than being indulgently constrained, that essence must be presented to the world through selfless channels. Virgo represents the feminine archetype of the Virgin Mother shielding her unborn child, of the Veiled Isis protecting her esoteric knowledge which is ineffably sacred.

That child is none other than the Christ Child, gestating within the confines of the womb, and ever protected by the veils of secrecy which separate secular knowledge from the Truth of the Absolute. This Truth has been secluded for centuries in monasteries, convents and mystery schools, with the intention of preserving its sanctity from the ignorance of the world.

Thus, Virgo esoterically carries an energy which symbolizes a mystical devotion to that which has become the ideal for perfection! This Christ Light, discovered in Leo, was taken in by the Virgin, the receptive female, and fiercely guarded. Cloisters flourished around this ideal, separating the spiritual from the secular, protecting the light from the darkness.

Within Virgo, then, there is that quintessential paragon, held high that it might not be tarnished. Yet, it is for Virgo to know that there must be a synthesis of the world of matter and the world of spirit, in order for this feminine sign to yield her bountiful harvest. There must be the holy marriage of inner and outer to bring forth the Christ Child. What was once religiously guarded in esoteric circles is now offered to all who seek it with purity of heart. It is none other than the story of Parsival and the Holy Grail.

This innate desire to protect the Holy Shrine is that which invokes within Virgo the impulse to offer herself in service to others. For, as Virgo initially pledged unswerving allegiance to the Grail, she must now turn and offer this same love to the masses. The love of the ideal must be brought into a practical reality and not secluded behind metaphoric abbey walls.

This is the underlying issue for Virgo, - to see that perfection exists in all things *as they are*, rather than to maintain a concept based upon an *historical ideal*. The nature of Virgo is to be overly critical, for she judges harshly that which does not meet her standards. This critical nature is induced by Virgo's inherent conflict over the synthesis of the secular and the spiritual.

The time has come for her to enter the world, to leave the cloister behind, and to establish for herself a sense of equality based on her *individual* contributions to society.

[33]

This basic need for equality provokes within Virgo a tendency toward an analytical and self-critical introspection, which is diffused externally by projecting those imperfections which she perceives within herself, onto others. Psychologically, this form of self-justification creates an illusion of security, while further distancing Virgo from the society into which she must integrate.

Virgo's analytical nature can create problems, for the ideal of perfection can blind her to all else. Thus, Virgo may never quite find that right job, the right mate, etc., until she opens herself to receive the beauty that the world offers.

A state of *synthesis is* reached as Virgo offers herself in service to others. *The sense of equality and placement in society*, Virgo's fundamental issues, will develop naturally as she balances the polarity between her disdain for imperfection, thus perceiving a lack of wholeness in her world, and her reverential humility which is engendered by her love of the Ideal, which consequently inhibits Virgo from seeing her own perfection!

[34]

In the process of becoming whole, this polarity must be synthesized, as a lack of integration tends to isolate Virgo, to create a sense of aloneness. As a distraction, Virgo will draw herself into relationships, many of them casual, in an attempt to alleviate this loneliness.

Virgo energy will manifest itself physically in a pristine beauty that can denote a certain purity of spirituality. The inner life has created the outer form, reflecting a time in which Virgo carried within herself the Child of Light.

Wherever Virgo lies within one's chart, there is the need to control the tendency toward excessive critical analysis and to create a synthesis, wherein a true sense of security can be reached through the knowledge that each of us carries the same light and we are, therefore, equal.

So it is for Virgo to place herself into the world, to synthesize her concepts of perfection with humility, and to create an inner wholeness, whereby the conceptual ideal is transmuted into the reality of worldly

[35]

love and service. As Virgo opens her heart to others, so does she to herself, and idealistic barrenness is transformed into fertility, as she begets the progeny of her wholeness. The Child of Light is carried forever in her heart and not within the mortality of the mind.

At this point, the soul has completed half of its journey through the Zodiac. The energies at play have related more specifically to the subjective world, and now, they begin an outward shift to the world beyond one's self.

Note: Mercury is the ruler of Virgo and the Sixth House which relates to work, health, small pets, mental or physical problems which result from internal conflict ("the mind is the slayer of the real"), and adjustment to the world at large. Virgo rules the intestinal tract.

"I Balance"

Cardinal   Air   Masculine   Venus   The Scales
Opal

"My feet will dance in liquid gold!
My head will float above earthly clouds!"

It is in Libra that the soul begins to initiate actions that relate to the world at large, particularly in the area of *relationships*. For now that one has passed through the subjective stages of development, it becomes important to relate to that which is not the personal self, to seek perspectives that do not emerge from within, and yet, to maintain one's individuality.

Thus, Libra is instinctively drawing itself into relationships of all kinds, wherein a certain balance of inner and outer realities

[37]

needs to be attained, through the act of giving and receiving. Not entirely freed from the lessons and energy of Virgo, Libra must also create a sense of equality based, not on social contribution, but on a *mutual reciprocity* of this energy, through partnership.

For within Libra, is a combination of the passive/aggressive dynamic that has the need to express itself in a balanced way. Libra's passivity, and a sometimes obsessive desire to please, has the potential to engender a certain martyrdom which can create anger in others. Likewise, Libra's aggressiveness is merely inner frustration over self-injustice, externalized in an Arian outburst. (It is to be remembered that Aries is the polarity to Libra.) It is essential for this equilibrium to be accomplished within Libra, before *true relationship* can be created. For this is none other than the merging of the inner male and female.

Although Libra is a masculine sign, the very components of its energy cannot preclude the feminine aspect as well. Thus it can be said that, in maturity, Libra is both

[38]

masculine and feminine, both passive and aggressive, and in the balancing of these energies, an androgynous harmony is conceived.

The feminine aspect of Libra is often externalized through a physical beauty that is softer than the aquiline perfection of Virgo. Additionally, there is an integral relationship with the aesthetic aspects of life. Libra loves beauty and its expression, whether through music, poetry, fashion, or art. There is a resistance to the unattractive qualities the world has to offer, as Libra will focus on that which is more pleasing to its artistic nature.

Libra's mind can soar through lofty realms, often lacking the ability to ground itself through action. It is common for Libra to initiate things on the mental plane, without necessarily bringing them to any conclusion. For Libra can vacillate between both sides of an issue, perceiving the just reality in each.

By its very nature, it is a social sign. Within Libra is a strong *social dynamic*, as its awareness has become more "we" oriented. This dynamic can initially express itself

[39]

superficially, drawing Libra into a series of seemingly insignificant relationships, for it cannot perceive itself without its "other half." On a deeper level, Libra seeks to attract to itself that which is necessary for its soul growth, the internal polarization of masculine/feminine dynamic.

The lesson for Libra is to maintain its individuality within a relationship, rather than losing itself to the other person, - to merge with another without diluting its essential uniqueness. Relationships purify the soul, teaching Libra to claim its individuality through the extremes of the passive/aggressive dynamic both within self and in partners.

Where Libra lies within the chart, there is the opportunity to balance the polarity of the masculine and feminine aspects of self and to reflect that balance through an *equal reciprocity* of giving and receiving in relationships, whether they are personal or professional. Here is also an area in which one can develop one's aesthetic nature.

In the merging of the active masculine and

passive feminine principles, Libra engenders within self the quality of Brotherly Love. Thus, Libra cultivates an inner sense of justice that can manifest externally through a balanced form of social and/or political activism.

The union of the higher and lower self (the soul and the personality) is none other than the Holy Marriage Libra has instinctively sought, wherein wo/man becomes complete within himself. Sequentially, Libra's outer world mirrors its natural state of balance, thus giving Libra the fundamental security of *individual equality* that is central to its needs.

Note: Venus is the ruler of Libra and the Seventh House which relates to relationships, marriage, open enemies, and the lower courts. Libra rules the kidneys.

Reflections of Consciousness

[42]

"I Penetrate / I Create"
Fixed   Water   Feminine   Pluto
The Scorpion/The Eagle/The Phoenix
Topaz   Malachite

"Through the deep and silent spaces
The sea of mystery enfolds us
On and on, forever on."

Lacking the social ease of Libra, Scorpio's energy is considered intense, as she carries within her a certain discomfort over the conflicting realities of a world that is largely superficial, and her own world which is vast and deep.

Essential to the nature of Scorpio is the desire to transcend the limits imposed by body-consciousness and to delve into the very mysteries of life! Inherent to this sign is

[43]

an insatiable curiosity, born of the need to penetrate and to fully understand all that comes under its piercing scrutiny.

Scorpio resonates strongly with issues surrounding love, sex, power, money, and death, and at some point she recognizes that they have a shadow side as well as a positive side. It is the destiny of Scorpio to learn the quality of discernment, for in her undeveloped stages, she can be mesmerized by the world of glamour and illusion and drawn into the murkier aspects of life.

As the Scorpion, there is a natural affinity for those darker mysteries which drive man to court danger and which accentuate his negative obsessions. There is a pull toward that which might be called the planetary underworld, - the realm of drugs, sex, power, and money used without a higher purpose.

However, this negative side to Scorpio is an *integral part of the whole*, and it must be transcended before the scorpion is transformed into the eagle, a higher vibrational aspect of this sign. In accordance with the particular evolution of the soul, this

[44]

drama is carried out through many levels of experience on both the physical and the astral planes. In many instances, the darker facet of Scorpio merely highlights a need to purify the emotional body.

Thus, time and time again, Scorpio will involve herself with people and experiences which will serve as catalysts for her *metamorphosis*. The possessiveness associated with this sign is an intense attachment to that which Scorpio is instinctively drawn for her transformation.

Her metamorphosis is often precipitated by an emotional shock, which ultimately forces her to release her attachment and to purify her emotional body. For it is the hypnotic power of desire which holds Scorpio to the lower vibrational planes. The natural course of action, subsequent to these upheavals is a period of complete withdrawal for personal regeneration.

At the center of Scorpio lies the dichotomy engendered by the nature of desire. This division is, in a sense, what separates Scorpio from the Self, as she ultimately struggles to

[45]

subjugate personal desire to the *will of the Soul*. Once this metamorphosis is complete, Scorpio begins the journey back to the Atman.

There is a deep sense of privacy surrounding Scorpio, who often prefers the comfort of seclusion to crowds. This can be inappropriately defined as secrecy, when the reality is that it distinguishes Scorpio's depth. Although this sign is known for its relentless penetration of others (giving excellent potential for criminal law), Scorpio can protectively maintain an inscrutable barrier for herself.

Somewhat resistant to change, it is not a sign of spontaneity. Nor is it one in which there is an openness to others, until a level of trust has been generated. At the first sign of betrayal, Scorpio will retreat, closing down all channels of communication. This sign is deeply impressionable, tormented by its own emotional storms and by the insensitivities of others. A negative projection of this sensitivity is the tendency to lash out with some form of revenge, verbal or otherwise.

[46]

Scorpio: *October 22 - November 22*

The sexual reputation Scorpio has acquired is really relative to the vibrational level of the one who is working with the energy of this sign. Generally speaking, there is a vital interest in the sexual area at an early age, before any bias has been developed. This attraction is propelled by an innate curiosity surrounding that which is considered to be "forbidden fruit", for this area is either totally ignored, or avoided by parents until a child has reached a certain level of maturity.

Fundamental to the nature of Scorpio is the need to *penetrate*, in order to know. Sexual union is not only a literal form of penetration, it is also a vehicle for transformation. Through sexual merging, Scorpio not only learns how two souls can access one another on an intensely deep level, but also how to acquire an understanding of one of life's greatest mysteries. When Scorpio begins to utilize its higher vibrational energies, the sexual union is regarded with greater respect, for there is an underlying awareness of the connection two souls make through this particular union, which may well later have

[47]

karmic repercussions.

The energy of Scorpio is not an easy one with which to work. Wherever it lies within the chart, there is a need to access one's *inner power through positive channels*. There are three symbols related to Scorpio - the Scorpion, the Eagle, and the Phoenix - allowing one to call on the energies of each for purification and metamorphosis. Often there is a fourth symbol correlated with Scorpio, and that is the Serpent.

For with the energy of Scorpio, comes admittance to all of the secrets behind the tapestry of life, - to the mystery schools, to the occult, to death itself, - and it is the allegorical Serpent who releases the fire which carries the knowledge and wisdom to Scorpio.

Thus, under the sign of Scorpio, the Path of Discipleship begins. It is the path along which one dies to the world of illusion and glamour, through the process of detachment and *right use of power*. The rebirth is into one's true nature in which is the embodiment of all that is most powerful in man, for it relates to his *very life force*. At this point, in the evolutionary

[48]

journey, the allegorical Serpent offers its apple, wherein Scorpio might satisfy its deeply inquisitive nature.

Note: Pluto the planet of transmutation and metamorphosis rules Scorpio and the Eighth House which relates to legacies, death, the occult, one's personal limits, others' resources, sex, and regeneration. Scorpio rules the generative system and the rectum.

Reflections of Consciousness

[50]

"I Perceive / I Aspire"

Mutable   Fire   Masculine   Jupiter   Centaur

Malachite   Amethyst

"The stars will guide me through the night
Fly me away on beams of light!"

Following the metamorphic energy of Scorpio, which has a contractile aspect to it related to the sign's fixity and its need to internalize everything, the focus again shifts outward via the energy of Sagittarius. For the *first* time, an expanded sense of awareness is born, and with it the recognition that there is indeed a world beyond the personal self, *and* that it is very large. Thus, in Sagittarius, a more comprehensive understanding comes about, related to this awareness and

[51]

correlative to all experiences or desires which support it.

The energy of Sagittarius is not self-contained, or fixed. Rather, it is optimistically adaptable to that which life presents, going with the flow as it were, with little clinging to events or to people, as they weave in and out of one's life experience. Freedom becomes the keynote to all that is Sagittarian in scope, for through this new expansiveness, comes the recognition that the world is composed of a diversity of lifestyles, thought systems, and people, and that an entire galaxy comes with it.

With this in mind, Sagittarius projects himself outwards, distance being no inhibitor, to participate in all that life presents. One element of this freedom is travel. Exotic places and faraway lands beckon, and if for some reason they remain inaccessible, then reading or philosophical pursuits become the options which will engender the expansiveness of Sagittarian energy. However, the greatest element of freedom, in particular for this sign, is the pursuit of all that which is the

Truth. Regardless of prison walls or open spaces, it is the *Truth which sets one free!*

Through Gemini, the polarity sign, the approach to life was to gather as much information, and as many concepts, as possible. With Sagittarius, there is the need to synthesize that which has been assimilated and to bring forth that truth which pertains to one on an *individual* basis. It is for Sagittarius to create his own ideology, without respect to that which the world ascertains to be true.

It might be that this truth can then be presented through the written word, allowing others their respective freedom to align with this, as they so choose. There is also a natural attraction to law, or the higher courts, in which the truth may again be revealed and presented for the benefit of others.

However, Sagittarius must recognize that that which he proclaims to be his own truth may not necessarily apply to those around him. There is a tendency toward dogmatism wherein Sagittarius, burning with the fire of revelation, may perceive such to be the truth

[53]

for all. Sequentially, this opinion would be imposed on others, without due respect for their individuality.

Thusly, Sagittarius must expand beyond his own perception and recognize that the Greater Truth is what binds all souls while, individually, the voice of Truth speaks in many tongues. Wherever Sagittarius is positioned within the chart, the door stands open, allowing one to cross the threshold beyond one's perimeters, into the Greater Story. There is the chance to transcend the mundane and to embrace the Ideal. As symbolized by the centaur, Sagittarius may leave the lower realms and shoot for the stars, transforming human consciousness into cosmic consciousness!

The words sage and sagacity relate to the wisdom inherent in the energy and name of this sign. Through the paths of understanding and compassion, one who works with this energy has the potential to expand his awareness into an all encompassing state. As freedom comes into play through the development of ideals, Sagittarius sees the light and, thusly, becomes the light, exemplifying those ideals which others can use as guidelines for their own growth. The Tao is accomplished through the synthesis of mind and heart, that a rightful balance between spiritual and personal ideals, and secular responsibility be maintained.

Note: Jupiter, the planet of expansiveness and of the auric body, rules Sagittarius and the Ninth House, which relates to long journeys, publishing, higher ideals, the intuitive mind, religion, and philosophy. Sagittarius rules the arteries, blood, the hips, and the thighs.

Reflections of Consciousness

"I Use"

Cardinal   Earth   Feminine   Saturn   The Goat

Jet   Sapphire   White Onyx

*"The greatest courage is to draw
wisdom from one's Self, -
That which is unsupported and free."*

Assuming that the natural law, pertaining to the individual, has been established in Sagittarius, the modus opperandi would be for him to *express* his truth by giving it form *in the world*, via Capricorn. The very nature of Capricorn embodies the composite of all that is the best and the worst in man, for Capricorn archetypically corresponds to the world of structure and form *and* to one's relative freedom within it.

This energy relates to our Universal laws of

Time and Space, even to the process which we call death. So it might be said that one begins to feel the energy of Capricorn, and its ruling planet Saturn, at a very early age. At some point in his development, the child will become aware of its own mortality. Until this significant moment, there is little reticence, and much bravado, over that which he can accomplish. When, through personal experience or information coming from an inner level, the awareness of death emerges, a shift occurs in which a certain fear is engendered, bringing with it a conceptual awareness of the limitations imposed upon him by these laws of time and space. This fear is an innate provocateur for those working with the energy of Capricorn.

One cannot speak of Capricorn without also speaking of its ruling planet Saturn, for throughout life's course, it is Saturn which can be one's greatest challenge and, ultimately, one's greatest ally. Saturn is the Lord of Karma, the Dweller on the Threshold. He, alone, has control over that gateway which remains closed to all of those who have not successfully passed the tests and re-sponsibilities which are essential to the evolutionary progress of the soul.

Once the requirements have been met, one is allowed to cross the threshold which will separate him, once and for all, from the masses. He will begin to access, and utilize, more refined energies. At this point, one begins to proceed on the path which is related specifically to his individual needs. Liberated from the restrictions of mass consciousness, one begins to prepare his individual destiny.

Thus, the energies of Capricorn present a particular test of responsibility for those who are working with them. If is often said that those who are born under the sign of Capricorn are far too serious, and yet, they are merely feeling the weight of this responsibility, no longer clearly under-standing, and often negating the child within.

It is common for those who are working with the lessons of Capricorn, to be strongly attached to the world of structure. This allows them a context in which to express their responsibility, simultaneously giving them a

[59]

sense of security no longer offered through the freedom they once experienced as children. For within the cellular make-up is the memory of that moment when the awareness of death annihilated the joy of immortal freedom, replacing it with a fear of the unknown.

It is also relevant to the nature of Capricorn to give rise to depression, for this ultimately forces one to give pause for introspection, initiating the potential for change. Were it not for this, Capricorn would find, within self, a certain crystallization of form transpiring, the outer and inner worlds mirroring one another. For this sign relates to governments, politics, and the laws which bind them together. In the physical world, these represent the manifestation of man's inner world of concepts and structure.

To look at Capricorn from another perspective, one must recognize the power inherent within its energy. It is through the utilization of this power that man either binds himself further to the Wheel of Karma, or that he liberates himself into his individuated state. Regardless of direction, this power must be expressed, for the repression of this energy engenders an anger which erupts within the body and which can demonstrate itself through several types of illnesses.

Correlative to Capricorn in the Tarot Deck are the Devil and the Hermit. The former represents wo/man's bondage to the illusion of the world of form. The latter represents one who allows his truth (found in Sagittarius) to be the beacon which guides him through the pitfalls and the often solitary Path of Life.

It is the *courage* to stand with this truth, *unsupported by others*, which liberates Capricorn from the herd. The goat then rises above all others in his ascent to the top of the mountain, whereupon he begins his trek upon the path of initiation. The mountain top experiences in the Bible, et al, relate to the Initiation, through Capricorn, in which one assumes the mantle of responsibility, and the freedom of individuated consciousness.

Thus, where Capricorn lies within the chart, know that there are trials to be endured, all of them related to overcoming

[61]

the bondage of fear which holds us back, so that we find our place in the world in accordance with natural law. The seemingly endless delays are merely aids which give strength to that purpose, that our inherent truth is in alignment with Universal Law, thereby releasing us from the Wheel of Karma.

Herein, Saturn ceases its role as formidable opponent and disciplinarian and steps into the roll of the Angel of Presence, ever there for guidance.

Note: Saturn the Great Cosmic Parent, rules Capricorn and the Tenth House which relates to placement in society, government, politics, one's particular work, and the parent of the same sex (or more dominant parent). Capricorn rules the knees and the skeletal system (structure).

There is also a relationship to the skin. Through many readings, this person has observed that, where there has been a misuse or even a repression of Capricorn energy in another life, the skin often manifests this through eruptions, particularly the type of acne which creates lesions. This can be transformed through proper channeling of this blocked energy via the planet in one's chart which relates to Capricorn, or through the house which has Capricorn on its cusp.

Reflections of Consciousness

"I Know"
Fixed   Air   Masculine
Saturn   Uranus   The Water Bearer
Amber   Opal

"Love weaves the golden threads of Destiny."

In Aquarius, there is the potential to begin working with more refined energies associated with the individuation process. This is the only sign that is ruled by two planets, Saturn and Uranus. The co-rulership corresponds to man's inherent nature, - his attraction to structure, or the known, and his innate curiosity to that which is the unknown. In Aquarius, the choice is offered, whereby one can remain within the limits of the safety zone imposed by the mind, and Saturn, or

[65]

whereby one may transcend these limitations to begin the return journey through the unknown to the Absolute.

It is for Aquarius to take the final leap, dropping all attachments to concepts and belief systems, manifested externally in the world of form, and to move beyond them to receive that which is new for the *evolution of mankind*. Consequently, this sign is often associated with detachment, as it pulls back to objectify its surroundings. In the immature Aquarian, this detachment can be a defense mechanism against the alienation it may feel in the world, and in relationships. With maturity, the inclination to detach stems from the need to perceive the truth from a completely objective perspective.

An internal sense of frustration often exists at the core of Aquarius, as it feels the pull toward freedom, while at the same time wishing to remain within its own state of security. In the Aquarian child, even the adult, this frustration can be expressed through terrific bouts of anger, often stupifying those who do not understand its source. For at times Aquarius' perception bleeds through into other dimensions, giving insight that most people can neither relate to nor understand. Unable to integrate his perception into others' reality base, Aquarius can be met with rejection, or ridicule, thus pushing him back into the security of secular limitation. Aquarius is to know that, through rejection, comes the necessary self-determination to push him beyond his own perimeters, into new growth.

This ability to move into a different reality can give Aquarius a sense of aloneness, in a world from which he can become increasingly isolated. (From others' perspective, the term "out there" would apply to Aquarius!) However, the lesson for Aquarius is to transform frustration into compassion, for he needs to boldly step into this isolation before he can offer his gift. This alienation is the commencement of Aquarius' evolution into a higher level of consciousness.

Aquarius must find a way to override the discomfort in being different. He is to know that the Saturnian element to his personality is the *world grounding him.* For it is the destiny of Aquarius to turn back, with *unconditional love* and compassion, to a world which may reject him, that he might offer the new knowledge he has received, that he might bear the gift of spiritual understanding, feeding others with the water of life.

It is the one who dares to be different who will ultimately lead society in new directions. Following the lesson in Capricorn, where one moves into the world with his truth, Aquarius must take this one step further, breaking away from the crystallization of the world into the *freedom of the unknown!* Through the polarity of Leo, the Light emerged. That Light left its idealized state in Virgo, went through the "dark night of the soul" in Scorpio, lead one to his own truth in Sagittarius, and incorporated itself in the world in Capricorn. It is for Aquarius to give this same Light, this very Truth, back to the world through the context of planetary service!

Feelings of alienation notwithstanding, Aquarius' attention is very much on the group. His ability to have many friends, in a detached sense, gives Aquarius the opportunity to objectify his perspective in focusing on that which the world needs. Equipped with a strong compassion for humanity, engendered by the development of self-awareness and other-awareness on the Zodiacal wheel, Aquarius begins to understand that he cannot progress alone. *All of humanity must evolve with him.*

Wherever Aquarius lies within the chart, there is the chance to detach, and to objectify, to bring forth a new sense of freedom and unconditional love. The tendency to hang onto feelings of isolation can be transformed by the comprehension that, although the road to freedom carries a great price, the nature of freedom is the very *essence* of each man, woman, and child!

Note: Saturn, the Cosmic Parent, and Uranus, the Awakener, co-rule Aquarius and the Eleventh House, which relates to one's friends, wishes and dreams, goals, and objectives. Aquarius rules the ankles, the circulation, and relates to the body's "electrical system" through Uranus.

"I Believe"

Mutable   Water   Feminine   Neptune   The Fish
Amethyst   Chrysolite

"Windswept, I lose my form in Thee."

At the entry point of the Zodiac, through
Aries, the soul's issues and experiences relate
to "Who am I?" With the completion of the
wheel in Pisces, the emphasis moves from the
personal self to the *search for God*. In Aries,
Consciousness entered the physical plane
and endured the trials related to a third
dimensional reality, as it became the Zodiacal
traveller. In Pisces, Consciousness initiates
the momentum toward releasing attachments in the world, while beginning the
process of being reabsorbed into itself.

[71]

With the soul's journey around the wheel in a state of near completion, Pisces, then, is a *composite of all the signs that preceded it*. This gives it an empathetic quality, whereby it can relate to all of the issues and feelings others may express, without having to personally experience them, for these issues are a part of Pisces' cellular memory.

However, the point in question for Pisces is to determine that which is specifically related to itself, for in a world that is attached to its identity to all things, Pisces finds its denouement in the issues surrounding *self-identification*. The mutability of the sign allows Pisces to adapt to its surroundings, yet the formlessness of the element of water prevents Pisces from creating its own perimeters.

Thus, Pisces struggles to know itself as a separate entity when, in truth, this type of discernment is next to impossible. However, there are a few options. One is to align with a stronger aspect within the chart, assuming that energy and avoiding Pisces all together. The other is to polarize itself through Virgo,

[72]

maintaining a balance through discrimination and the identity associated with serviceable work.

The ultimate focus for Pisces is to aspire for that state, wherein the ego consciousness has been dissolved into the Whole. The nebulous quality of this sign can create an escapist tendency, where Pisces would lose itself in drugs, alcohol, etc. in order to avoid the reality in which it must live.

For with Neptune as its ruling planet, Pisces has more than enough affinity for the world of illusion. Neptune oversees this realm, which encompasses drugs, alcohol, film, glamour, and all that the world offers as a smoke screen to prevent one from perceiving beyond it to the greater reality. Neptune also *IS* the greater reality!

With its empathetic quality, Pisces draws to itself those who seek counseling for problems, as Pisces understands all that which is inherently a part of its own self. It can absorb that which surrounds it, even *becoming* it, transcending natural boundaries, where Pisces can no longer define its perimeters. Because there is an inability for self-discernment, Pisces may refrain from making decisions or commitments, frustrating others who claim to see the picture with more clarity.

Thus, in the journey through the Zodiac, the soul evolves through the knowing of itself in relationship to the karma it has chosen to work out. The completion is in Pisces, yet there is also the greatest potential to perceive the world through myopia. In a sense, it's the last chance to indulge in the illusory reality, before the soul's fusion with the Absolute.

Pisces is very sensitive, very impressionable. Wherever it lies within the chart, there is the need to see beyond the illusion it may create for itself. There is the need to look across the chart to Virgo, to use this sign as a helpmate in developing discernment and self-definition. Mysticism, self-sacrifice, healing, counseling, and compassion are all tenets for this sign. There is also the promise of eternal fulfillment that does not come from the physical reality.

For the other side of Pisces presents an

entirely different reality, - the Christ (or Cosmic) Consciousness. Herein, mankind must make the choice, for it is not forced upon him. If Pisces' greatest aspiration is Christ Consciousness, then the energy of its ruling planet, Neptune, will surely dissolve one, until there is no longer the illusory screen between the one and the ONE. It is here in which the true reality becomes the transformation of consciousness into the Absolute, wherein all perception, all separation, all duality ceases, - where the only truth is "I AM!"

Note: Neptune, the Great Dissolver, rules Pisces and the Twelfth House which relates to seclusion, mysticism, hidden enemies and karma, the unseen, drugs, illusion, film, secrets, self-sacrifice, and the subconscious mind. Pisces rules the feet.

Epilogue

Thus the soul has completed its cycle through the Zodiac. It will invariably return, entering through various signs to fulfill its individual mission in relation to the Whole. Years ago, as wee ones, we played a game in which, through the pointing of a finger, our identities were given to us. It went: "Rich Man, Poor Man, Beggar Man, Thief. . .Doctor, Lawyer, Indian Chief." So this little game sums up the evolution of the soul as it assumes a multitude of personas in the Great Game of Life. Eventually, everyone gets to play the King, the Queen, the Beggar, the Fool. That the role of the Beggar is more charmed than that of the King is solely determined by the attitude of the player.

REFLECTIONS OF CONSCIOUSNESS
*Share the experience
of this astrological gem with
your friends and family*

Also by the same author
DARK PLACES, LIGHT PLACES
A novel of love . . . and grace

Mysteriously smuggled from China at birth, raised in a secluded monastery in France, Etienne's spiritual life unfolded with grace. However, his beloved teacher was unable to protect him when the shadows of the Revolution became his rite of passage into the Light.

ORDER FORM